When I grow up I want to be a tiger

When I grow up I want to be a tiger

written by prerna singh bindra
illustrated by maya ramaswamy

SPEAKING TIGER

SPEAKING TIGER PUBLISHING PVT. LTD
4381/4, Ansari Road, Daryaganj,
New Delhi–110002, India

First published in India by Speaking Tiger in hardback 2017

Copyright © Prerna Singh Bindra 2017
Illustrations copyright © Maya Ramaswamy 2017

ISBN: 978-93-86582-08-9
10 9 8 7 6 5 4 3 2 1

Design & Layout by Pranav Capila, Second Skin Media
Printed at

All rights reserved.
No part of this publication may be reproduced, transmitted, or stored in a retrieval system, in any form or by any means, electronic, mechanical, photocopying, recording or otherwise, without the prior permission of the publisher.

This book is sold subject to the condition that it shall not, by way of trade or otherwise, be lent, resold, hired out, or otherwise circulated, without the publisher's prior consent, in any form of binding or cover other than that in which it is published.

Dedicated to
all tiger cubs – may
they grow up to be
tigers, and reign over
the wilds – and to all
those who protect them

I am a tiger cub. I am just six months old.

We are wild animals, and don't have names, but you can call me T-Cub.

Sometimes, my sister, silly girl, calls me 'Happy' because I am *always* smiling.

I live in a forest in India. It's called Baghvan.

It has big trees, bigger hills and the biggest playground of grass, and lots of water – that runs, and runs! It's a river, Ma says.

Water is fun. One day I looked in the river and saw another little tiger in it.

I smiled. He smiled back. I jumped. He jumped as well!

Copy Cat Tiger, I thought and hit him. **SPLASH**. He hit me back!

"Silly you," said my sister, "that is you. Your image in the water."

HUH?

Ma explained that was my *reflection*.

So now, I often go to the river to check how much I have grown, and if my whiskers are growing longer and longer.

In my forest there are many birds and animals. They are all so different!

Wood-peckers that go **tak-tak-tak**, tapping old trees with their strong beaks.

Hornbills with large yellow beaks and great wings that say ***whoosh-whoosh*** when they fly.

There are big black bears who dig in the sand with their pointy nails.

There are strong sambar deer wearing a crown of antlers, and also elephants!

Elephants are big – bigger than *everything*. They have big ears and a very long nose called a trunk. When I saw one, I thought an angry cloud was running after me. I got scared and hid behind my Ma.

The elephant had a baby – and she hid behind her mother as well!

I like langur monkeys. Langurs are funny animals with small black faces and long tails. They can jump very high and even walk up a tree!

Once, I tried to catch a langur's tail, but he climbed up a tree – high, higher, right to the very top. I tried to follow him, but I fell down – **thwack!**

It's fun to scare peacocks and see them run helter-skelter with their fancy tails.

I like to chase butterflies, too.

But most of all, I love to play with my sister. We chase each other, stalk as if we are hunting, and even mock-fight. Sometimes Ma joins us, and that is the *best*.

Playing is a fun way to practice being grown-up. It also makes us agile and strong!

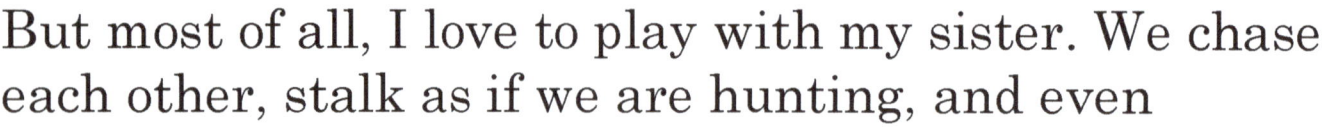

One night Ma decided that we should learn how to hunt for our food.

There are so many animals in the jungle that we can hunt — deer, wild pigs, monkeys, hare and sometimes even the mighty elephant.

But isn't it cruel, Ma? No, she said, they are our food. If we don't eat some of the deer, they will eat all the grass and plants and the jungle will become bare and brown, and slowly die.

My Ma, she is very wise.

Also all that talk about food made my stomach growl!

We had our first hunting lesson. I was so excited!

I am all grown-up now, I thought. I huffed and puffed my chest and roared loudly:
AAAUNNGH!

"Silly," said my sister, "Ma asked you to keep *quiet*."

All that noise alerted the wild pigs. They grunted and rumbled and ran. I came back with my tail between my legs.

I will do it next time, I thought. I will be still and silent and catch my prey by surprise.

But then I forgot to hide in the tall grass and the deer saw us and ran away!

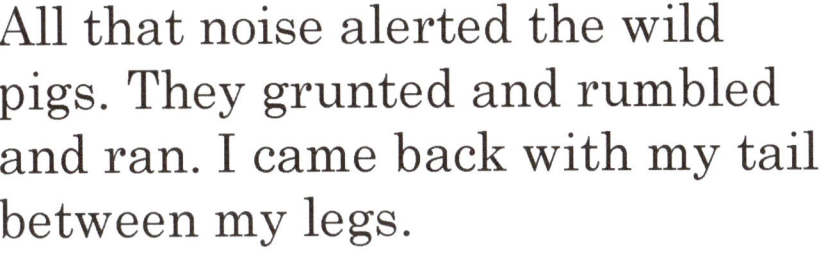

Once, I tried to kill a big sambar deer and he attacked me with his antlers!

I was scared, but mother came to my rescue and frightened the sambar away.

In the forest, my Ma is the *strongest*.

Ma gave me a big whack for not listening to her. "You are still too young, son. Don't go near big animals," she growled.

"And never, ever go near Humans. They are not jungle animals. It is wise to fear them. Sometimes people can be cruel; they might hurt you."

"But why?" I asked. Ma thinks I ask too many questions!

Ma explained that our skins are beautiful and our bones are strong. So some greedy people – poachers – kill tigers and sell them in the market.

"Why?"

"Because some foolish people believe that eating our bones will make them strong like us. T-Cub, you be a smart boy, stay in our forest, and stay away from people," she said.

"Yes", I said, "I love my forest. And am I not a Tiger, the King of the Jungle, and bigger and stronger than Man?"

"Yes you are, my pet," said Ma, "stronger than everyone on earth, but men become powerful because they have weapons like guns that can kill.

"Watch your step, son. It is not easy being a tiger. There are dangers everywhere."

I resolved to be safe, and brave.
Because, when I grow up,
I want to be a tiger.

I was also *very* scared.

So I hugged my mother and pulled my sister's tail.

We climbed trees and slipped and chased a poor langur monkey. We had lots of fun and I smiled again!

Then one day, I lost my smile.

Ma had gone hunting. Sometimes we went with her. Sometimes she went alone. Sometimes she came back quickly with yummy food. Sometimes she told us to follow her where she had hidden our dinner. Sometimes she came back after hours and hours, with no food.

One day, she did not come back.

The sun came up, and went down. Yet she did not come back.

We were so hungry, so thirsty and so scared.

Where was Ma? Why was she not coming back?

I wanted to run and search for her, but where? Where in this vast forest would she be? Had she ventured outside the forest?

How would I find her? Where? And Ma had told me never to go anywhere alone…

And I always listen to Ma. *Really*.

Scary thoughts troubled my sister and me.
Had Ma been hit by a bullet?

Ma had told me I must watch my step when I walk, because sometimes bad people – poachers – set traps, which catch our legs: **SNAP!** It hurts and hurts. And most times we cannot break free. Maybe Ma didn't watch her step?

I also thought of those metal monsters with the big mean eyes that glow, which run like mad and crush us forest creatures. Maybe they crushed her?

What if my Ma were dead?!

I was very scared and sad. I was also very hungry.

But I couldn't hunt because I'm still too small and the deer is too big.

So I started to cry. It was the first time I cried, and my sister became even more frightened, so we hugged and tried to shut our eyes, and the nasty thoughts, away.

The sun came up, it was bright and sunny. And still no sign of Ma.

We had almost given up hope…

Then after a long, long time, I heard a soft step… and smelled a familiar smell…

*Aaaaaungh...
Aaaaungh...*

"T-Cub?" purred a gentle voice. "My dear, dear cubs…"

Ma? Ma? **MAAA!**

She looked so tired, hurt and woeful. I saw that she was limping. Her paw was red. It was bleeding.

I knew then that she had been caught in a trap, but she came back to us. I wondered how. But this time, I did not ask any questions.

All I cared was that my Ma was **BACK!** With us!

We jumped around her in joy and hugged her and rubbed her face with ours (that is how we tigers kiss), and I think she was happy again.

My mother came back and so did my smile!

ABOUT TIGERS

T-Cub is special. All tigers are. They are the most powerful and largest of all cats in the world. They are also one of the loudest! Their roar can be heard over a few kilometres. They can live in dry forests such as those found in Rajasthan, thick evergreen jungles like in Arunachal Pradesh and Myanmar, in the wet mangrove forests of the Sundarbans (India-Bangladesh), and also in snowy mountains in Far East Russia and Bhutan.

You can recognise tigers by their stripes! Each tiger is unique and has its own pattern. Tigers are the only cats who love water. In the summer, they will cool off in ponds and streams, very much like you do in swimming pools or village ponds!

Cubs are born blind, just like little kittens. Tiger moms are devoted and fiercely protect their cubs. Tigresses are single mothers – the father doesn't play a role in bringing up cubs, though he may visit them frequently. A tigress keeps her cubs clean (by licking them), carries them (by the scruff of their neck), and brings them food to eat. As they grow older, she takes them around the forest and teaches them to hunt. The cubs stay with their mother until they are about two years old, and then wander off to find their own patch of forest, to raise their own families.

This cycle of life has continued for millennia. Tigers have roamed the earth – all across Asia from Turkey in the west to the eastern coast of Russia – for over two million years.

But now they are in trouble. Tigers are endangered. There are only about 3,800 wild tigers in the world. Tigers are strictly protected, and it is against the law to hunt them. Even so, bad people – poachers – illegally hunt and kill tigers for their skins to make luxury coats and rugs. Tiger bones are illegally sold for very high prices as medicine in some countries, where people falsely believe it will cure them of diseases.

The other big problem is deforestation. Tigers need large, undisturbed forests to live, roam, hunt and bring up their cubs. People are clearing away forests, cutting the trees and the vegetation to make cities and fields, and also factories, buildings, roads, mines, dams and many such things. Tigers have already lost over 90 percent of their forests! We must save the precious forests that are left, if we are to save tigers.

You may ask: But why save tigers at all? As apex (top) predators, tigers are at the top of the food chain, their presence indicates a healthy forest. Forests are the lungs of the earth, providing oxygen. They provide another great service to people by storing carbon, and so are called 'carbon sinks'. As trees grow, they absorb carbon dioxide from the atmosphere and store it in their trunks, branches, roots. This helps fight global warming. Forests also nourish soils, which is vital for us to grow food. Many rivers and streams originate from forests, and we all know that water is life! Today, many cities and villages in India do not have clean water because forests are being cut down.

I also think tigers are very beautiful, and the Earth is as much their home as it is ours.

Tigers are the soul and the spirit of the forest.

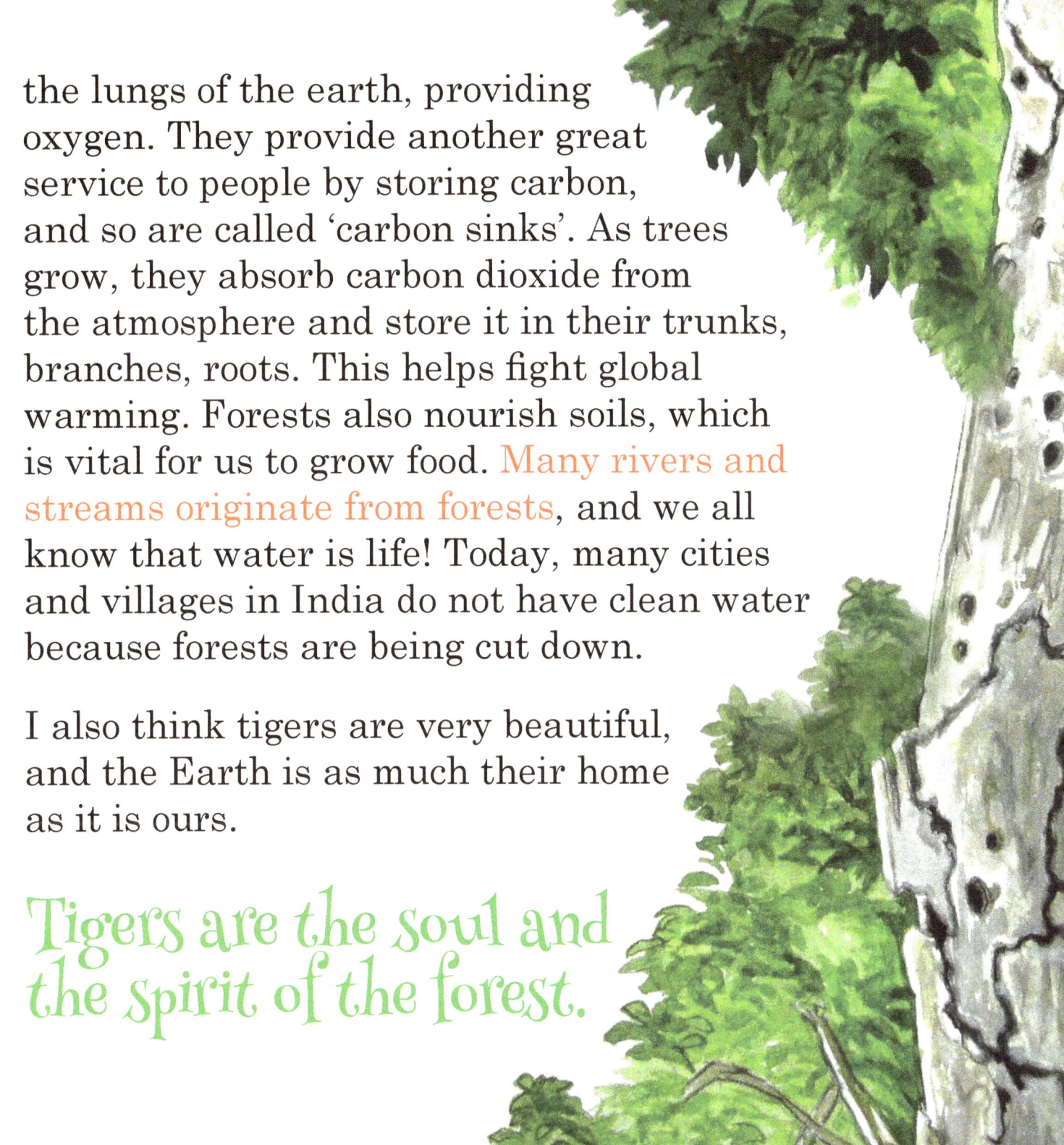

SAVING TIGERS

Do you want to help T-Cub grow up to be a tiger? Here's what you can do:

Knowledge is power: Read books, see films, talk to people working in this field and learn about tigers and wildlife. Become aware of the problems and threats to tigers, and why they are important.

Speak up for tigers: They can't speak for themselves. (They can roar and growl though!) Be their ambassador, talk about tigers to your family, friends, in your school. Let people know that tigers are on the brink of extinction, why, and how they can be helped. Tell them why tigers matter.

Support those who protect tigers: There are many good people like forest guards and rangers, who

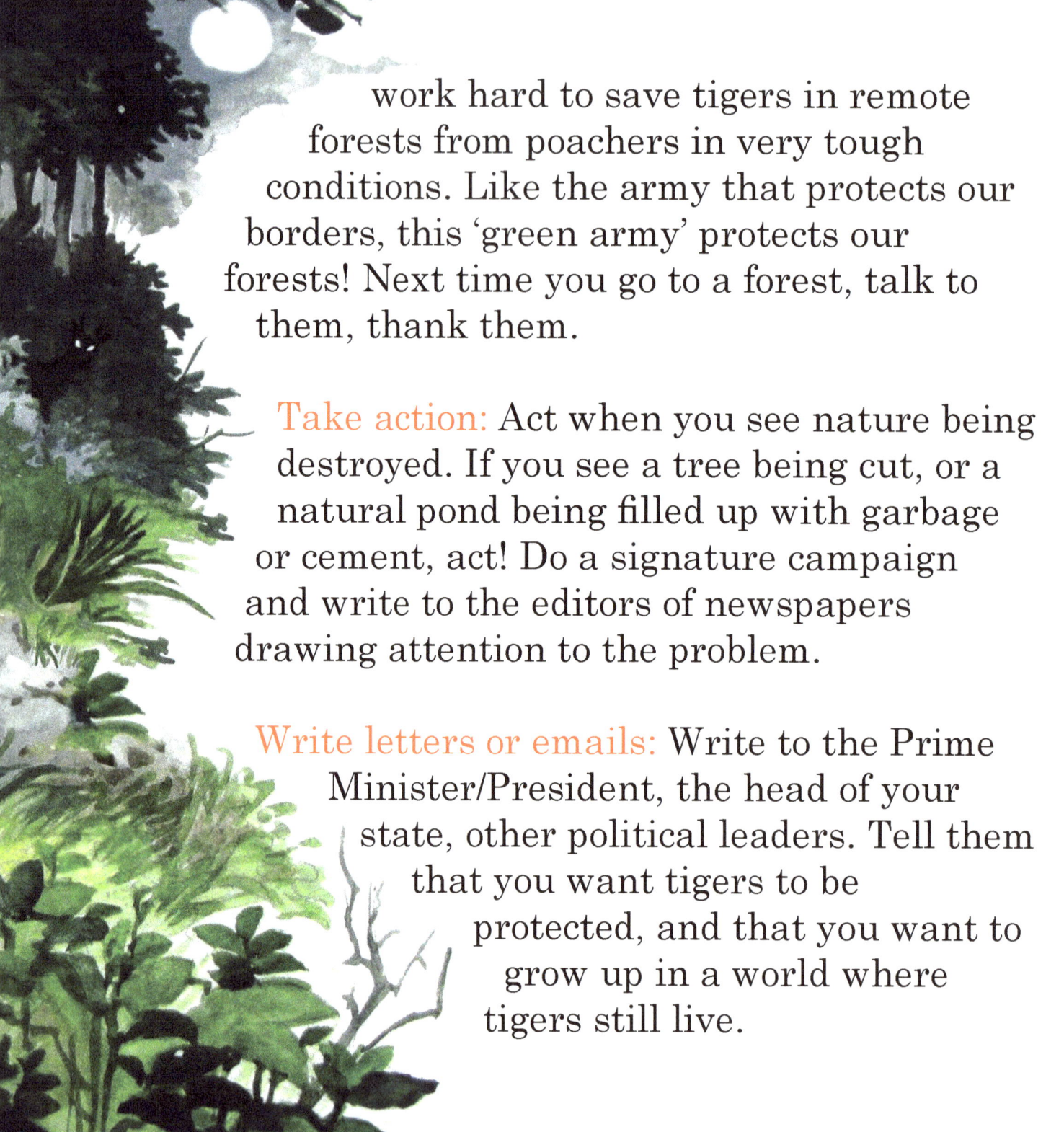

work hard to save tigers in remote forests from poachers in very tough conditions. Like the army that protects our borders, this 'green army' protects our forests! Next time you go to a forest, talk to them, thank them.

Take action: Act when you see nature being destroyed. If you see a tree being cut, or a natural pond being filled up with garbage or cement, act! Do a signature campaign and write to the editors of newspapers drawing attention to the problem.

Write letters or emails: Write to the Prime Minister/President, the head of your state, other political leaders. Tell them that you want tigers to be protected, and that you want to grow up in a world where tigers still live.

Start a Nature Club: Get together with your friends in your school and society. Go for nature walks and bird watching. Read (and share!) books on wildlife, nature. Organise nature film shows.

A suggested activity: Find out if there is a water shortage in your city. With the help of your parents or teachers, try locating your city's water sources on a map and see where most of your water comes from. For example, Mumbai is one of India's most crowded cities, yet it also has a thick forest in its midst – Sanjay Gandhi National Park. The park is the catchment area for two lakes – Vihar and Tulshi, which supply water to Mumbai. A catchment area is land where water collects when it rains. The forest absorbs rain like a sponge, then releases it slowly into streams, and rivers, ensuring there is water all year through. Without forests to soak the water and release it bit by bit, it will simply flood everywhere – in the fields, in the cities, roads.

And if you are in Mumbai, visit Sanjay Gandhi

National Park. Go on a nature trail. Other cities also have forests and green spaces around. Find yours!

Raise funds: Raise money for NGOs or people working for wildlife. Make greeting cards, bake cookies, and sell. I know someone who polished shoes, another who passionately told people how very few tigers were left, and raised money for tigers! They have both grown up to be big supporters of wildlife.

Be a good citizen of Planet Earth: Refuse. Reuse. Recycle. Save resources: Shut off lights when you don't need them, turn off taps. Think before you buy things: Do you really need them? It seems like small stuff, but when you save the earth's precious, limited resources, you lighten the burden on forests and other natural habitats from where they are sourced. And you are helping save tigers.

Be a responsible tourist: Visit forests. Watching wildlife is an amazing experience. But don't forget that you are guest in the tiger's home.

I always think of forests as a holy place, like a temple, and treat it with respect and awe. Don't litter. Be silent. Listen, instead, to the exciting sounds of nature. Don't chase tigers (in jeeps) or any other wild animal. Open your eyes, and your heart, to nature… and you are in for an exciting journey of discovery.

Part of the proceeds of this book will be donated for conserving tigers, and other wildlife.

Books to Read on Tigers & Wildlife

I hope T-Cub has kindled in you a curiosity about tigers and the natural world. As a child I lived in a city and there really was no one who would take me to jungles. But my family was into reading and it got me into the habit too! It was books that first inspired me and got me involved with wildlife. They opened my eyes to the animals around me: I would try identify the birds in my garden, protect the peacock eggs in the shrubs in the nearby compound, wonder about the bats that hung upside down from trees.

Here are a few of my favourite books, and authors:

James Herriot does not write on wildlife, but I fell in love with dogs thanks to his books, and understood that animals have feelings and personalities, too.

Gerald Durrell's books are such fun, and will take you to forests around the world. Get your hands on, and laugh out loud with his **My Family and Other Animals**.

Ruskin Bond's writings on nature and animals are delightful. You have lots to catch up on if you haven't read Uncle Ruskin. Start with **Friends in Wild Places** published by Speaking Tiger.

Read **Ranjit Lal**'s books on nature, adventure and wildlife. They will make you smile, and think, and wonder.

Jim Corbett taught me a lot about natural history, though I didn't like the hunting bit.

Start reading **Cub magazine**, it's published by Sanctuary Asia, and they even have a programme, 'Kids for Tigers', that you could get involved in. And start writing for **Cub magazine** as well! Check out their website.

Michael Morpurgo is another author whose work I enjoy.

I have also been very inspired by the writings of **M Krishnan** and **F W Champion**, and of course **Rudyard Kipling** and his wonderful **Jungle Book**!

Prerna Singh Bindra

lives in a city, but is usually found wandering in forests, where she may get to meet tigers, elephants and other animals. She is a writer, a keen student of nature and a wildlife warrior who wants to save all wild animals and the wildernesses they live in.

Prerna has played a role in protecting many pristine forests and is a strong voice for endangered wildlife. She dreams of a world where people are not "at war with nature", but respect and value nature, where children retain their innate sense of wonder and there still exist wildernesses for them to explore.

Prerna's very best friend is her dog, Doginder Singh.

Maya Ramaswamy

is a wildlife artist based in Bangalore, India.

A keen student of natural history and conservation, she worked as a volunteer for wildlife conservation as a schoolgirl. She has illustrated several books for Katha and Pratham Books.

Maya is inspired by natural India. "We must preserve the rich tapestry of our wild and natural habitats, wetlands and protected areas if we hope to preserve the health of water, soil, and ensure food security for future generations," she says. "Our children cannot laugh on barren lands full of man-made clutter."

ALSO FROM SPEAKING TIGER

FRIENDS IN WILD PLACES
BIRDS, BEASTS AND OTHER COMPANIONS

Ruskin Bond

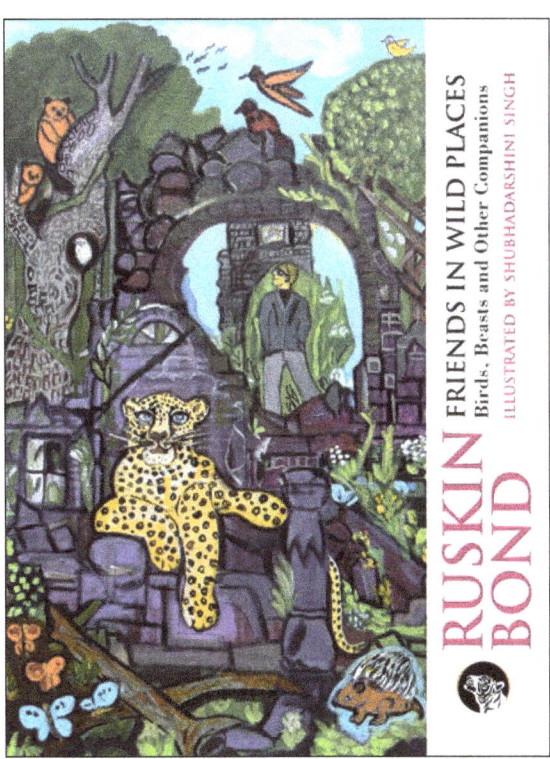

"Below my cottage was a forest of oak...Nearly every morning, and sometimes during the day, I heard the cry of the barking deer. And in the evening, walking through the forest, I disturbed parties of Kaleej pheasants. I saw pine martens and a handsome red fox. I recognized the footprints of a bear. As I had not come to take anything from the jungle, the birds and animals soon grew accustomed to my face."

Since he was a young boy, Ruskin Bond has made friends easily. And some of the most rewarding and lasting friendships he has known have been with animals, birds and plants—big and small; outgoing and shy. This collection focuses on these companions and brings together his finest essays and stories, both classic and new. There are leopards and tigers, wise old forest oaks and geraniums on sunny balconies, a talking parrot and a tomcat called Suzie, bears in the mountains and kingfishers in Delhi, a family of langurs and a lonely bat—and many more 'wild' friends, some of an instant, others of several years.

Beautifully illustrated by Shubhadarshini Singh, this is a gift for nature- and book-lovers of all ages.

www.ingramcontent.com/pod-product-compliance
Lightning Source LLC
Chambersburg PA
CBHW061142230426
43663CB00028B/3001